HENRY KISSINGER

The Definitive Biography and Untold Story of a Diplomatic Giant

Richard Biden

Table of Content

Introduction

In the corridors of power, where history is forged and destinies shaped, there are figures who transcend their time, leaving an indelible mark on the course of nations. Henry Kissinger is one such enigmatic luminary, a diplomat, and statesman whose name echoes through the annals of modern American history. With his cunning intellect, unyielding determination, and a diplomacy that could navigate the most treacherous international waters, Kissinger was a geopolitical maestro.

In this biography, we embark on a journey through the life of a man whose very name is synonymous with the art of statecraft. With each turn of the page, you will venture behind the scenes of diplomacy's inner sanctum, where the stakes are global, the tensions palpable, and the decisions consequential.

This biography is not a mere recitation of facts; it is an exploration of the human behind the statesman's mask. It delves into the complexities of a figure who has both been hailed as a visionary diplomat and criticized as a Machiavellian puppeteer. But whatever your preconceptions about Kissinger may be, be prepared to see them challenged.

We will unravel the enigma of a young refugee from Nazi Germany who would rise to become one of the most influential Secretaries of State in American history. From the hallowed halls of Harvard University to the smoky back rooms of Washington, you will follow Kissinger's trajectory, a journey that encompasses Cold War brinksmanship, secret missions to Beijing, and the intricate dance of diplomacy in the Middle East.

But this biography aims to be more than just a recounting of historical events. It is an exploration of the man's essence, his motivations, his ideals, and his flaws. It delves into the controversies that continue to swirl around his legacy and questions whether the ends can ever truly justify the means in the realm of geopolitics.

With exhaustive research and a deep understanding of the political landscape, this book strives to paint a portrait of Henry Kissinger that is as vivid and intricate as the man himself.

Prepare to embark on a journey through the corridors of power, a journey where decisions are made, alliances are forged, and where one man's influence reverberates through the annals of history.

Chapter 1

Early Life and Background

Family and Childhood

Heinz Alfred Kissinger entered the world on May 27, 1923, in Fürth, Bavaria, Germany. He was born into a family of German-Jewish heritage, with his mother Paula (née Stern) and father Louis Kissinger. The family roots traced back to the adoption of the surname "**Kissinger**" by his great-great-grandfather, Meyer Löb, in 1817, inspired by the Bavarian spa town of Bad Kissingen.

In his formative years, young Kissinger's life was a blend of ordinary childhood experiences and a burgeoning passion for soccer. He became a member of the youth team of SpVgg Fürth, one of Germany's premier football clubs at the time.

Immigration to the United States

The trajectory of the Kissinger family's life took a significant turn in 1933 when Adolf Hitler was elected Chancellor of Germany. This watershed moment sent shockwaves through the Kissinger family, prompting a fundamental reevaluation of their future. As Nazi rule solidified, Kissinger and his friends faced regular harassment and assaults by Hitler Youth gangs. The young Kissinger occasionally defied the racial segregation imposed by Nazi laws by sneaking into soccer stadiums, an act that often resulted in brutal encounters with security guards.

The dire consequences of Nazi anti-Semitic laws manifested in Kissinger's inability to gain admission to the Gymnasium, the German secondary school, and his father's dismissal from his teaching position.

On August 20, 1938, when Henry Kissinger was just 15 years old, he, along with his family, embarked on a perilous journey to escape further persecution. Their journey included a brief stop in London before they arrived in the bustling harbor of New York City on September 5th.

Education and Early Ambitions

Resettled in New York City, Kissinger attended high school in the Washington Heights neighborhood, a vibrant hub for the German-Jewish immigrant community at the time. While he assimilated quickly into American culture, his distinct German accent persisted, rooted in a childhood shyness that often made him hesitant to speak.

After completing his first year at George Washington High School, Kissinger embarked on an unusual journey. He began attending school at night, simultaneously working at a shaving brush factory during the day to support himself and his family.

Upon graduating from high school, Kissinger enrolled at the City College of New York, initially focusing on accounting. His academic prowess shone even as he worked part-time. However, his studies were interrupted in early 1943 when he was drafted into the U.S. Army.

Call to Service (U.S. Army)

When Henry Kissinger enlisted in the U.S. Army, his journey took him to Camp Croft in Spartanburg, South Carolina, for basic training. It was here, on June 19, 1943, at the age of 20, that he officially became a naturalized U.S. citizen, solidifying his commitment to his new homeland. Initially, the army directed him to study engineering at Lafayette College in Pennsylvania. However, fate intervened when the engineering program was canceled, leading to Kissinger's reassignment to the 84th Infantry Division.

In the 84th Infantry Division, Kissinger's intellect and fluency in German caught the attention of fellow immigrant Fritz Kraemer. Recognizing Kissinger's potential, Kraemer facilitated his placement within the division's military intelligence section. In this role, Kissinger would not only experience the rigors of combat with the division but also step forward willingly for hazardous intelligence duties, particularly during the harrowing Battle of the Bulge.

As the American forces advanced deeper into Germany, an unusual opportunity arose. Kissinger, despite holding the lowest military rank of private, was entrusted with the administration of the city of Krefeld. This decision stemmed from a critical lack of German speakers among the division's intelligence staff. Remarkably, within a mere eight days, Kissinger had established a functional civilian administration, demonstrating his resourcefulness and administrative skills.

His remarkable journey continued when he transitioned to the Counter Intelligence Corps (CIC). Here, he ascended to the rank of sergeant and was tasked with leading a team in Hanover, charged with the crucial mission of tracking down Gestapo officers and other saboteurs. In recognition of his exceptional service, he was honored with the Bronze Star for his contributions.

In June 1945, Kissinger assumed the role of commandant of the Bensheim metro CIC detachment in the Bergstrasse district of Hesse. In this capacity, he bore the immense responsibility of overseeing the denazification process in the district. Despite wielding extensive authority and the power of arrest, Kissinger demonstrated a commitment to treating the local population fairly and with respect, avoiding any abuses of power during his command.

Following his separation from the army, Kissinger's dedication to intelligence and education persisted. In 1946, he embarked on a new chapter, teaching at the European Command Intelligence School located at Camp King, a role he continued as a civilian employee. This marked the beginning of his transition from military service to the academic and diplomatic spheres, setting the stage for a career that would ultimately shape American foreign policy.

Henry Kissinger's military service not only showcased his valor but also laid the groundwork for his future contributions to the world of politics and diplomacy.

Chapter 2

Academic and Scholarly Pursuits

Academic Achievements

Henry Kissinger's academic journey was marked by extraordinary achievements, laying the foundation for his future diplomatic and scholarly endeavors. He completed his undergraduate education at Harvard College in 1950, where he earned a Bachelor of Arts degree with summa cum laude honors and was inducted into the prestigious Phi Beta Kappa honor society. During his time at Harvard, he resided in Adams House and had the privilege of studying under the esteemed scholar William Yandell Elliott.

One of the early glimpses into Kissinger's scholarly prowess was his senior undergraduate thesis titled *"The Meaning of History: Reflections on Spengler, Toynbee, and Kant"*. This remarkable thesis exceeded 400 pages in length, setting a standard that still influences academic writing with its impact reflected in the current word limits for academic works.

Further enriching his academic journey, Kissinger pursued advanced degrees at Harvard University, earning both his Master of Arts and Doctor of Philosophy degrees in 1951 and 1954, respectively.

Early Writings and Publications

While still in the early stages of his academic journey, Kissinger's intellectual curiosity led him to contribute significantly to the fields of international relations and political thought. In 1952, during his graduate studies at Harvard, he served as a consultant to the director of the Psychological Strategy Board. Simultaneously, he founded the thought-provoking magazine

16

"**Confluence**", demonstrating his early interest in the fusion of ideas and international relations.

Notably, during this period, Kissinger contemplated working as a spy for the Federal Bureau of Investigation (FBI), showcasing his willingness to engage in matters of national importance.

Kissinger's doctoral dissertation, titled *"Peace, Legitimacy, and the Equilibrium (A Study of the Statesmanship of Castlereagh and Metternich),"* stands as a pivotal work in the development of his scholarly insights. In this dissertation, he introduced the concept of "legitimacy" in international relations, a notion that would profoundly influence his later diplomatic strategies. He defined "legitimacy" as an international consensus on the nature of workable diplomatic arrangements and the permissible goals and methods of foreign policy. For Kissinger, an international order accepted by all major powers was "legitimate," while an order not accepted by one or more great powers was considered "revolutionary" and therefore perilous.

Kissinger's exceptional dissertation earned him the Senator Charles Sumner Prize, an accolade reserved for the most outstanding dissertations produced by students under the Harvard Department of Government.

Kissinger's academic journey continued at Harvard, where he served as a faculty member in the Department of Government. He also played a pivotal role as the director of the Harvard International Seminar from 1951 to 1971. In 1955, he consulted with the National Security Council's Operations Coordinating Board and worked as a study director in nuclear weapons and foreign policy at the Council on Foreign Relations. It was during this period that he released his book *"Nuclear Weapons and Foreign Policy,"* which challenged the Eisenhower Administration's nuclear doctrine of "massive retaliation".

Simultaneously, he authored "**A World Restored**" in the same year, delving into the dynamics of balance-of-power politics in post-Napoleonic Europe.

From 1956 to 1958, Kissinger assumed the role of director for the Rockefeller Brothers Fund's Special Studies Project. His commitment to academic excellence continued as he directed the Harvard Defense Studies Program from 1958 to 1971, co-founding the Center for International Affairs with Robert R. Bowie. He served as the associate director of the Center for International Affairs and embarked on consultative roles with government agencies and think tanks, including the Operations Research Office, the Arms Control and Disarmament Agency, the Department of State, and the RAND Corporation.

Keen on influencing U.S. foreign policy, Kissinger became a foreign policy advisor to the presidential campaigns of Nelson Rockefeller, supporting his Republican nomination bids in

1960, 1964, and 1968. His fateful encounter with Richard Nixon at a social gathering in 1967 marked a significant turning point. Initially skeptical, Kissinger soon recognized Nixon's potential and offered his support, eventually serving as National Security Advisor after Nixon's election as President in 1969.

Chapter 3

Rise in Government

Entry into Government Service

Henry Kissinger's journey into government service marked a pivotal chapter in his career, as he transitioned from academia to the corridors of power. In 1955, while still deeply immersed in his academic pursuits at Harvard, Kissinger ventured into government service as a consultant to the director of the Psychological Strategy Board. This initial foray into the realm of national security and strategic planning hinted at the significant role he would play on the global stage.

Kissinger's aptitude for policy analysis and strategic thinking quickly became evident during this period, foreshadowing his influential future as a diplomatic thinker and advisor.

National Security Council

Kissinger's career trajectory took a momentous turn in 1969 when he was appointed as the National Security Advisor by President Richard Nixon. This pivotal role made him the principal architect of U.S. foreign policy and national security strategy, setting the stage for a remarkable era in American diplomacy.

As the National Security Advisor, Kissinger wielded immense influence in shaping U.S. foreign policy during a tumultuous period of history. His tenure coincided with significant global events, including the Vietnam War, the Cold War, and the opening of diplomatic relations with the People's Republic of China.

Kissinger's intellectual prowess and strategic acumen came to the forefront as he worked closely with President Nixon to navigate complex international challenges. His efforts culminated in the formulation of the Nixon Doctrine, which emphasized the need for U.S. allies to take greater responsibility for their own defense. This doctrine aimed to recalibrate America's global commitments and redefine its role in a changing world order.

Under Kissinger's guidance, the National Security Council became a hub of strategic thinking, where critical decisions were made, and policies were crafted with a deep understanding of global power dynamics. His diplomatic endeavors extended beyond traditional state-to-state relations, encompassing groundbreaking efforts in diplomacy and conflict resolution.

Kissinger's leadership at the National Security Council was characterized by pragmatism, intellectual rigor, and a commitment to advancing U.S. interests in a complex and interconnected world. His influence reached far beyond the confines of the White House, extending to the international stage where he engaged in shuttle diplomacy and high-stakes negotiations.

Chapter 4

Diplomacy during the Cold War

U.S.-Soviet Relations

The Cold War era was marked by intense geopolitical rivalries, ideological conflicts, and the ever-present specter of nuclear annihilation. It was during this tumultuous period that Henry Kissinger, as the National Security Advisor and later as the U.S. Secretary of State, played a pivotal role in shaping U.S.-Soviet relations. His diplomatic finesse and strategic acumen became critical instruments in navigating the treacherous waters of superpower competition.

At the heart of Cold War diplomacy was the U.S.-Soviet relationship, a high-stakes game of chess played out on a global scale. The ideological chasm between the capitalist West and the communist East set the stage for a protracted conflict where the world often teetered on the brink of nuclear war.

Kissinger's approach to U.S.-Soviet relations was characterized by realpolitik, a pragmatic and realistic view of international affairs. His belief in the importance of balance-of-power politics guided his diplomatic efforts. Kissinger recognized that stability could be achieved by engaging the Soviet Union in negotiations and agreements rather than solely through confrontation.

One of the most notable achievements of Kissinger's diplomacy during the Cold War was the Strategic Arms Limitation Talks (SALT). These negotiations resulted in the SALT I Treaty, signed in 1972 by the United States and the Soviet Union. The treaty placed limits on the number of intercontinental ballistic missiles and submarine-launched ballistic missiles, effectively curbing the nuclear arms race and reducing the risk of nuclear conflict.

Additionally, Kissinger's secret negotiations with Soviet Ambassador Anatoly Dobrynin, often held in unconventional locations such as a New York apartment or a quiet park bench in Washington, played a crucial role in defusing tensions during critical moments of the Cold War. These "backchannel" communications allowed for candid discussions and paved the way for important agreements, including the Incidents at Sea Agreement and the Basic Principles Agreement.

Kissinger's engagement with the Soviet leadership, including General Secretary Leonid Brezhnev and Foreign Minister Andrei Gromyko, demonstrated a keen understanding of Soviet motivations and sensitivities. His ability to establish a level of trust and mutual respect was instrumental in opening channels of communication during an era of deep mistrust.

While the U.S.-Soviet relationship remained fraught with ideological differences and periodic crises, Kissinger's diplomatic endeavors contributed to a more stable and predictable superpower dynamic. His strategic thinking and negotiation skills helped reduce the risk of catastrophic conflict, providing a glimmer of hope during the darkest days of the Cold War.

Opening Relations with China

A defining moment in the history of international diplomacy occurred when Henry Kissinger, as the National Security Advisor to President Nixon, embarked on a groundbreaking mission to open relations with the People's Republic of China. This diplomatic overture would not only reshape the Cold War landscape but also alter the course of global politics.

For years, the United States had no official relations with the communist government of China. The Sino-Soviet split, a rift between the two communist giants, offered an opportunity for Nixon and Kissinger to explore a historic realignment of U.S. foreign policy. The Cold War doctrine of containment, which had guided U.S. policy for decades, was undergoing a profound transformation.

Kissinger's secret visit to Beijing in 1971, known as the "ping-pong diplomacy," marked the initial thaw in Sino-American relations. This covert mission paved the way for President Nixon's historic visit to China in 1972, an event that captured the world's attention.

The strategic calculus behind this diplomatic maneuver was twofold. First, it aimed to exploit the growing schism between China and the Soviet Union, leveraging the "China card" to gain an advantage in the ongoing Cold War competition. Second, it sought to forge a new alignment to counterbalance the Soviet threat. Kissinger's ability to engage in delicate and discreet negotiations with Premier Zhou Enlai and Chairman Mao Zedong was instrumental in establishing the framework for rapprochement.

The Shanghai Communique, a joint statement issued by the United States and China in 1972, outlined their common interests and the shared goal of peace in Asia. It also acknowledged the existence of one China, a fundamental principle of Chinese foreign policy.

The implications of opening relations with China reverberated across the globe. It represented a diplomatic masterstroke that altered the dynamics of the Cold War. The United States now had an additional player on the global stage, and the triangular diplomacy between the U.S., the Soviet Union, and China introduced new complexities into superpower relations.

Furthermore, the normalization of relations with China had profound economic and cultural impacts. It set the stage for increased trade, people-to-people exchanges, and the eventual integration of China into the global economy. The China-U.S. relationship evolved into one of the most significant bilateral relationships of the modern era.

Kissinger's role in this diplomatic breakthrough was pivotal. His ability to navigate the complexities of U.S.-Chinese relations, foster trust with Chinese leaders, and craft a strategic framework for cooperation represented a testament to his diplomatic skill and foresight. The opening of relations with China remains one of the enduring achievements of his diplomatic legacy, with ramifications that continue to influence contemporary geopolitics.

In this chapter, we have explored the intricate and high-stakes world of Cold War diplomacy, where Henry Kissinger's realpolitik approach and his pivotal role in opening relations with China played a transformative role in shaping the course of history. His contributions to U.S. foreign policy during this era reflect a remarkable blend of strategic thinking and diplomatic finesse, leaving an indelible mark on the global stage.

Chapter 5

Secretary of State Under Nixon and Ford

Appointment and Early Initiatives

Henry Kissinger's appointment as the U.S. Secretary of State under Presidents Richard Nixon and Gerald Ford marked a defining moment in American diplomacy. As the nation's top diplomat, he navigated the turbulent waters of international relations during a period of profound geopolitical shifts and global challenges.

Kissinger assumed the role of Secretary of State in 1973, having previously served as the National Security Advisor to President Nixon. His transition to the State Department represented a significant elevation in his influence over U.S. foreign policy.

One of his early initiatives was to restructure and reform the State Department, aiming to enhance its capacity for strategic thinking and policy planning. Kissinger recognized the need for a more integrated approach to foreign policy, ensuring that diplomacy and statecraft were aligned with U.S. national interests and objectives.

Moreover, Kissinger's approach to diplomacy was characterized by pragmatism and realpolitik, an emphasis on practical considerations and the pursuit of national interest. This approach would become a hallmark of his tenure as Secretary of State.

Vietnam War and Southeast Asia

The Vietnam War presented one of the most complex and challenging issues during

Kissinger's tenure as Secretary of State. As the United States sought an honorable exit from the conflict, Kissinger played a central role in negotiations with North Vietnam.

Kissinger's secret negotiations with North Vietnamese negotiator Le Duc Tho in Paris, resulting in the Paris Peace Accords in 1973, marked a significant milestone in the U.S. withdrawal from Vietnam. The accord led to a ceasefire and the release of American prisoners of war. Kissinger's shuttle diplomacy and ability to manage the delicate negotiations were instrumental in bringing an end to U.S. involvement in the Vietnam War.

However, the peace achieved in Vietnam remained fragile, and the subsequent collapse of South Vietnam in 1975 marked a deeply contentious chapter in U.S. foreign policy. The legacy of the Vietnam War would continue to shape American diplomacy and influence policy decisions for years to come.

Kissinger's diplomatic efforts extended beyond Vietnam to address the broader dynamics of Southeast Asia. He sought to stabilize the region, prevent the spread of communism, and maintain U.S. influence. His engagement with countries such as Thailand, Cambodia, and Laos played a crucial role in shaping the geopolitical landscape of Southeast Asia.

Détente and Middle East Diplomacy

Kissinger's tenure as Secretary of State coincided with a significant period of détente in U.S.-Soviet relations. Building on his earlier diplomatic efforts during the Nixon administration, Kissinger worked to ease Cold War tensions and establish a framework for peaceful coexistence between the superpowers.

One of the key achievements of détente was the Strategic Arms Limitation Talks (SALT II) negotiations. These talks, aimed at limiting nuclear arms, resulted in the signing of the SALT II Treaty in 1979. While the treaty faced challenges in the U.S. Senate and was never ratified, it symbolized a commitment to arms control and reducing the risk of nuclear confrontation.

Kissinger's diplomatic outreach extended to the Middle East, where he played a pivotal role in addressing the Arab-Israeli conflict. The Yom Kippur War of 1973 had plunged the region into a crisis, and Kissinger's shuttle diplomacy between Israeli and Arab leaders was instrumental in brokering ceasefires and negotiations. His efforts culminated in the Camp David Accords in 1978, where Egyptian President Anwar Sadat and Israeli Prime Minister Menachem Begin signed a historic peace agreement. The accords marked a significant step toward peace in the Middle East and earned Kissinger the Nobel Peace Prize.

Kissinger's diplomatic leadership in the Middle East continued as he facilitated negotiations on the disengagement of forces in the Sinai Peninsula and the Golan Heights. His ability to bridge divides and build trust between longstanding adversaries showcased his diplomatic finesse.

In addition to his engagement in the Middle East, Kissinger's diplomatic endeavors extended to Africa, Latin America, and other regions, where he sought to advance U.S. interests and foster stability.

Chapter 6

Awards and Recognition

Henry Kissinger's contributions and recognitions extend far beyond his diplomatic career, showcasing his significant impact on various domains.

In 1973, he was jointly awarded the ***Nobel Peace Prize*** with Le Duc Tho for their work on the Paris Peace Accords, which led to the withdrawal of American troops from the Vietnam War. Le Duc Tho declined the award, deeming it incompatible with his beliefs and emphasizing that true peace had not yet been achieved in Vietnam. Kissinger, in a display of humility, donated his prize money to charity, refrained from attending the award ceremony, and even offered to return his prize medal following the fall of South Vietnam to North Vietnamese forces 18 months later.

Over the course of his lifetime, Kissinger garnered various awards in recognition of his contributions to public service. In 1973, he received the **_U.S. Senator John Heinz Award_**, acknowledging him as the individual who had provided the most outstanding public service among elected or appointed officials. In a rather unique tribute, Kissinger was granted the distinction of becoming the inaugural honorary member of the Harlem Globetrotters in 1976.

His contributions were also acknowledged by President Gerald Ford, who awarded Kissinger the **_Presidential Medal of Freedom_** on January 13, 1977. The year 1980 saw Kissinger win the **_National Book Award in History_** for the initial volume of his memoirs, titled "The White House Years".

In 1986, he was among twelve distinguished individuals who received the Medal of Liberty. His international recognition included being named an honorary Knight Commander of the

Most Distinguished Order of St Michael and St George in 1995.

Kissinger's enduring impact on public life continued as he received the ***Sylvanus Thayer Award*** at the United States Military Academy at West Point in 2000. In 2002, he was honored with honorary membership in the International Olympic Committee.

Israel acknowledged Kissinger's significant contributions by presenting him with the ***President's Medal in 2012***. Following that, in October 2013, he was honored with the ***Henry A. Grunwald Award*** for his dedication to public service by Lighthouse International.

Kissinger's involvement extended to academia, as he was a founding member of the council of the Rothermere American Institute at the University of Oxford.

He remains an active member of several prominent organizations, including the Aspen

Institute, Atlantic Council, Bilderberg Group, Bohemian Club, Council on Foreign Relations, Center for Strategic and International Studies, World.Minds, and Bloomberg New Economy Forum.

In the corporate realm, Kissinger served on the board of Theranos, a health technology company, from 2014 to 2017. He was also recognized with the Theodore Roosevelt American Experience Award from the Union League Club of New York in 2009 and assumed the role of Honorary Chair for the advisory board of the Bloomberg New Economy Forum in 2018.

Kissinger's contributions to society were further celebrated with the *__Ellis Island Medal of Honor__*. Most recently, in 2023, he was bestowed with the *__Bavarian Maximilian Order__* for Science and Art by Minister-President of Bavaria Markus Söder. These honors and acknowledgments underline his enduring influence and multifaceted contributions to diplomacy, academia, and public service.

Chapter 7

Critics and Controversies

Opposition to Kissinger's Policies

Henry Kissinger's illustrious career was not without its share of detractors and critics. While he was widely respected for his contributions to diplomacy and international relations, there were those who vehemently opposed his policies and approaches to foreign affairs. This chapter delves into the various forms of opposition and criticism that Kissinger encountered during his tenure as U.S. Secretary of State and beyond.

Kissinger's Realpolitik approach to foreign policy, characterized by a focus on pragmatic and national interest-driven decisions, drew both admiration and censure. One of the major points of contention was his handling of the Vietnam

War. As the principal architect of the Nixon administration's policy in Vietnam, Kissinger faced fierce opposition from anti-war activists, scholars, and even some political figures who believed that the U.S. should have withdrawn from Vietnam earlier to avoid further bloodshed and destruction.

Kissinger's secretive and clandestine diplomacy during the Vietnam War negotiations in Paris also raised eyebrows. Critics accused him of prolonging the conflict and causing unnecessary suffering by delaying peace talks for political gain. His diplomatic strategies, including the so-called "Christmas Bombing" of North Vietnam in 1972, were harshly criticized as excessive and inhumane.

Furthermore, Kissinger's involvement in the U.S.-backed coup in Chile in 1973, which led to the overthrow of President Salvador Allende and the rise of General Augusto Pinochet, sparked outrage and condemnation. Many viewed this intervention as a violation of Chilean sovereignty and an affront to democratic principles.

Kissinger's support for authoritarian regimes in countries like Argentina and Iran, where human rights abuses were rampant, also attracted intense opposition. Critics argued that his policies prioritized geopolitical considerations over human rights and democratic values.

His approach to the Middle East, particularly his role in the 1973 Arab-Israeli war and subsequent negotiations, generated mixed reactions. While some lauded his efforts to broker ceasefires and peace agreements, others accused him of bias and favoritism toward Israel.

Allegations of War Crimes

One of the most persistent and serious controversies surrounding Henry Kissinger has been the allegations of war crimes and human rights violations. These allegations have been raised in connection with various aspects of his tenure as National Security Advisor and Secretary of State.

Kissinger's involvement in the secret bombing campaign in Cambodia during the Vietnam War was met with accusations of indiscriminate bombing and civilian casualties. Critics argued that the bombings violated international law and the Geneva Conventions. The secretive nature of the operation only fueled suspicions of wrongdoing.

The use of covert operations and support for questionable regimes in Latin America, such as Chile, Argentina, and Uruguay, led to allegations of complicity in human rights abuses, including torture and disappearances. These allegations tarnished his reputation and led to legal challenges in multiple countries.

In the case of East Timor, Kissinger's approval of military assistance to Indonesia during its invasion and occupation of the territory raised concerns about the U.S. government's role in human rights violations. The United Nations and human rights organizations accused Indonesia of widespread abuses during this period.

Perhaps the most contentious issue is the alleged U.S. involvement in the overthrow of Chilean President Salvador Allende in 1973. While Kissinger's direct role remains a subject of debate, declassified documents have suggested U.S. knowledge of and support for the coup. This has fueled allegations of U.S. interference in the internal affairs of a sovereign nation.

The continued legal and moral questions surrounding these actions have led some to advocate for investigations and potential charges against Kissinger for war crimes. While these allegations have not resulted in formal legal action, they have left a lasting mark on his legacy and contributed to the ongoing debate over the ethics of U.S. foreign policy during his tenure.

Henry Kissinger's career was marked by both admiration and strong opposition, with allegations of war crimes and human rights violations casting a shadow over his legacy. This chapter explores the complexities of his controversial tenure as a statesman and the enduring debates about the ethical dimensions of his foreign policy decisions.

Chapter 8

Personal Life and Relationships

Family Life

Beyond the world of diplomacy and politics, Henry Kissinger's personal life has been marked by a series of significant relationships and family dynamics. This chapter offers a glimpse into the private side of the renowned statesman.

Kissinger's journey into family life began in 1949 when he married Anneliese "Ann" Fleischer, who hailed from Fürth, Germany. Their union brought two children into the world, Elizabeth and David. However, the marriage eventually faced strains and challenges, leading to their divorce in 1964. This turning point marked a transition in Kissinger's personal life.

Friendships and Relationships

One of the most notable aspects of Henry Kissinger's personal life was his romantic involvement with Austrian poet Ingeborg Bachmann. Their relationship, which began in 1955, extended over several years and added a layer of complexity to Kissinger's private world. The connection between a prominent statesman and a celebrated poet is a testament to the multifaceted nature of Kissinger's life.

In a significant chapter of his life, on March 30, 1974, Kissinger embarked on a new journey when he married Nancy Maginnes. This marked a fresh start, and the couple has since made their home in Kent, Connecticut, and New York City. The marriage brought stability and companionship to Kissinger's life, and it's been a lasting partnership that has accompanied him through various phases of his post-government career.

Kissinger's son, David Kissinger, ventured into the world of entertainment and media. He served as an executive with NBC Universal Television Studio and later assumed the role of the head of Conaco, Conan O'Brien's production company, in 2005. David's career choices added a different dimension to the Kissinger family's legacy.

In a more personal note, in February 1982, at the age of 58, Henry Kissinger underwent coronary bypass surgery, highlighting his own mortality and the importance of health in his life. His successful recovery from this medical procedure allowed him to continue his pursuits in diplomacy, academia, and public service.

Remarkably, Henry Kissinger's life journey led him to the remarkable milestone of turning 100 years old on May 27, 2023. This centenary celebration is a testament to his resilience and the enduring impact he has had on the world stage.

As a concluding note, Kissinger's affinity for the game of Diplomacy, as he described it in a 1973 interview, offers a glimpse into his personal interests and preferences. This chapter highlights the intricate interplay between his public and private life, offering a more holistic understanding of the man behind the statesman.

Chapter 9

Legacy and Influence

Kissinger's Impact on U.S. Foreign Policy

Henry Kissinger's legacy in the realm of U.S. foreign policy is extensive and enduring. This chapter delves into the profound influence he exerted on the nation's approach to international relations and diplomacy, leaving an indelible mark on American foreign policy.

Kissinger's tenure as National Security Advisor and later as Secretary of State under Presidents Nixon and Ford was marked by a series of defining moments that shaped U.S. foreign policy. His role in opening diplomatic relations with China in 1971, after decades of estrangement, significantly reconfigured the global political landscape. The establishment of relations with the People's Republic of China not only served as a strategic counterbalance to the Soviet Union but also laid the groundwork for future economic and diplomatic ties between the two nations.

In the Middle East, Kissinger's shuttle diplomacy in the aftermath of the 1973 Yom Kippur War played a pivotal role in brokering ceasefires and initiating peace talks. His efforts led to the disengagement agreements between Israel and its Arab neighbors, contributing to a period of relative stability in the region.

Kissinger's realpolitik approach, which prioritized national interest and pragmatic diplomacy, significantly influenced subsequent administrations. The concept of "linkage," where various aspects of international relations were interconnected and used as leverage in negotiations, became a hallmark of his diplomatic strategy.

His negotiations to end the Vietnam War, culminating in the Paris Peace Accords in 1973, played a crucial role in facilitating the withdrawal of American forces from Vietnam. Though the peace was short-lived, it represented a significant milestone in the conflict.

Kissinger's contributions extended to arms control and the prevention of nuclear proliferation. His involvement in the Strategic Arms Limitation Talks (SALT) with the Soviet Union led to agreements that curtailed the arms race and reduced the risk of nuclear conflict.

Ongoing Relevance

Henry Kissinger's influence continues to reverberate in contemporary discussions of foreign policy and international relations. His realpolitik approach, which remains a subject of debate, is still cited and analyzed in the context of modern diplomatic challenges.

The Kissingerian model of diplomacy, characterized by pragmatism and a focus on national interest, has found application in numerous diplomatic initiatives. The concept of "shuttle diplomacy" and the use of backchannel communications have been employed by subsequent administrations in resolving complex international conflicts.

Kissinger's writings, including his books "Diplomacy" and "World Order," continue to be studied and referenced by scholars and policymakers. His insights into the balance of power, the role of diplomacy, and the challenges of a multipolar world remain relevant in the 21st century.

His work in promoting détente and arms control has left a lasting legacy in international efforts to manage nuclear weapons and reduce the risk of global conflict. The principles underlying these negotiations continue to inform discussions on non-proliferation and disarmament.

Kissinger's involvement in the Middle East peace process and the Camp David Accords between Egypt and Israel established a framework for subsequent negotiations in the region. His diplomatic achievements provide a historical backdrop for contemporary efforts to address the Israeli-Palestinian conflict.

In the realm of U.S.-China relations, Kissinger's early overtures and diplomatic groundwork have paved the way for the complex but critical relationship between the two global powers. His insights into the importance of managing this relationship and understanding China's historical perspective have informed modern U.S. foreign policy.

In summary, Henry Kissinger's legacy endures through the principles, strategies, and diplomatic methods that continue to shape U.S. foreign policy and international relations. His influence on how nations engage with each other, balance power, and pursue global stability remains a compelling and relevant subject of study and discussion in the modern era.

Conclusion

Henry Kissinger's life and legacy evoke a complex blend of admiration, controversy, and enduring influence. As we conclude this biography, it is essential to delve into the multifaceted nature of the man and his impact on the world of diplomacy and foreign policy.

Kissinger's journey, from a young Jewish refugee who fled Nazi Germany to becoming one of the most prominent figures in American foreign policy, is a testament to the possibilities that the United States has offered to countless immigrants. His intellect, drive, and determination propelled him from the hardships of his early years to the pinnacle of international diplomacy.

His tenure as National Security Advisor and Secretary of State under Presidents Richard Nixon and Gerald Ford marked a pivotal period in U.S. foreign policy. The realpolitik approach he employed, characterized by a focus on national interest and pragmatic diplomacy, redefined how the United States engaged with the world. His efforts to open diplomatic relations with China and his shuttle diplomacy in the Middle East are iconic achievements that continue to shape international relations.

Kissinger's legacy extends far beyond his time in government. His writings, including seminal works like "Diplomacy" and "World Order," offer a profound understanding of the dynamics of international politics and the challenges of our interconnected world. His insights into diplomacy, balance of power, and the complexities of managing a multipolar world remain invaluable resources for scholars, policymakers, and practitioners of international relations.

The enduring relevance of Kissinger's principles and strategies is evident in their application by subsequent generations of diplomats and leaders. The concept of realpolitik, the use of backchannel communications, and the importance of understanding the historical perspectives of other nations are just a few examples of his lasting contributions.

His pursuit of peace, epitomized by his involvement in the Vietnam War negotiations and the Camp David Accords, showcases the potential for diplomatic solutions in even the most intractable conflicts. His commitment to arms control and the prevention of nuclear proliferation continues to shape global efforts to safeguard peace and security.

Yet, Henry Kissinger's legacy is not without its share of controversies and criticisms. His realpolitik approach has faced moral and ethical scrutiny, with detractors arguing that it sometimes prioritized stability and national interest at the expense of human rights and justice.

Allegations of war crimes and human rights abuses during the Vietnam War and in the context of U.S. policies in Latin America have cast a shadow over his legacy. While supporters argue that he made difficult decisions in a complex geopolitical landscape, critics maintain that these actions should not be overlooked or forgotten.

In the final analysis, assessing the man and the legacy of Henry Kissinger is a complex endeavor. His contributions to international diplomacy, his impact on U.S. foreign policy, and his enduring influence on subsequent generations of diplomats and leaders are undeniable. Yet, his legacy also encompasses controversies and ethical dilemmas that raise questions about the choices made in the pursuit of geopolitical goals.

As we reflect on the life and times of Henry Kissinger, we are reminded of the intricate interplay between personal conviction and global responsibilities, between the pursuit of power and the quest for peace. His story is a reminder of the enduring complexities of the human experience, where ambition, intellect, and decision-making shape the course of nations and the destiny of individuals.

In the end, the man and his legacy will continue to be a subject of study, debate, and contemplation. Henry Kissinger's life and contributions remain a compelling narrative in the ongoing story of international relations and diplomacy.

Printed in Great Britain
by Amazon

34758826R00037